Twenty Something

Jessica Martyn

BookLeaf
Publishing

Presentation by *BookLeaf Publishing*

Web: www.bookleafpub.com

E-mail: info@bookleafpub.com

ISBN: 978-93-95784-99-3

First edition 2022

*To my parents, my partner and my soul
mate best friend for always embracing
every phase of me.*

Transition

I saw you just the other day
At least, you know, it feels that way
We made our plans to meet again
But never followed through

I knew you just a month ago
Shared stories only we could know
Of times when we felt less alone
When one had become two

I remember when we met
In a crowded bar without pretense
Though years have slipped away since then
I'm blessed to have known you

Some day we will meet again
And I will greet you as a friend
I know we won't have to pretend
At least this much is true

Black and White

If I am black and white, up and down, day and
night
Then you are everything in between
If I am everything I say once my mind has
snuffed its light
Then you are all the other things I mean
Wherever I am, you are not
It's easier that way
Some arguments are best forgotten
With nothing left to say

Between Us

Nothing but air between us
But over time, that air grows so thick, so dark
With the memories of all the times I could have
called
And I didn't

Miss you in the back of my mind
Only because the front is so often preoccupied
Thought the future would be us against the
world
But it isn't

Still search for your name online
Though we're no longer "friends"
Looking for the validation you used to provide
To the highest bidder

Thought I couldn't afford to lose
But maybe I just can't afford to keep you

Work

I want to
make you
happy

I want to
feel at
peace

But

This place is
not
conducive

To fulfilling
these needs

The walls are
lacking
colour

My soul feels
tired and
grey

Surely, I
am far
too young

To go
to work
today

Wanderlust

When you give up everything you know
What's left of you? Where do you go?
Anywhere you like.

When you say goodbye to closed-in walls
What will you lose? How far will you fall?
Fly and be free.

When you fear, deep down, what lies beyond
How will you go? What's already gone?
All the old lies.

When you let go of what you've assumed
What will life be? What will you do?
More than you need.

Presence

Born without a map without a path on which to
walk

Born into a world that muffles action under talk

Born to find myself when I don't know where to
start

Born to fall in love until I have a change of heart

Don't know where I'm going, but I'll find my
way somehow

Might get there someday, but first, I'll be here,
now

Travelling On

Grass grows over the road ahead
Long and winding cobblestone
Walk along, searching for an end
Only half realising that it's all wrong

In the end, only the journey remains
So go with the wind, run the "wrong" way
The meaning is often in unexpected places
found in small moments each day

Days Like These

Not once have I done this before
I have not loved like this before
Nor risen above like this before
Give me days like these, a thousand more

There are no answers in this book
And pages get no second look
If all we have are these four walls
Give me days like these, a thousand more

De Facto

I remember days of old when I was young and
you were bold
Your chest was warm, my hands were cold, but
you never complained – not once

You were the fire around which I gathered, and
yours were the words that truly mattered
When my steps faltered, and my heart shattered,
you never complained – not once

You'll always be my first real love – a love that
cuts through all the stuff
In an empty house, we filled our cup – and I'll
never complain about us

Self

Too big, too small, too much, too little
My body is soft but my self-esteem is brittle
But at least I know myself
At least, I think I do

It's not your fault, the doctors say
It's not your fault you feel this way
It's the media, see – just the way of the world
At least, we think it is

I tried to be thinner, and smarter, and better
But as my body shrunk, my head filled with lead
It's depression, you know – all your friends have
it, too
At least, they feel like they do

Whatever I am, I surmise this is true
That I am just as lost and broken as you
It's your twenties, they say, as they look down
their noses
At least, for now, it is

A Function of Time

Once upon a time, twenty-five was older
A functioning person with bills to pay and
responsibilities to shoulder
But now it's just
Me

Once upon a time, life was a theme park
Full of endless rides and games and buckets
filled with sugar
But now, the fun isn't
Free

Once upon a time, opportunities were endless
Young, dumb, and free, wandering down the
road without a care
But now, the time is
Short

Once upon a time, I had big dreams
I wanted things I'd never heard of, and things
I'd never seen
But now, I just want
Happy

The Journey

13

Where to next? The driver asks.
But I don't know, I've never known
And maybe I never will

He tries small talk, I try it too.
But I don't have any small thoughts
And maybe I never will

Stare out the window, don't look too close
Wonder what comes next though nobody knows
And maybe we never will

The Daily Grind

From golden glow to velvet sea
There is no time to simply be
The rush from one thing to the next
Will stop my heart and steal my breath

They say "slow down", I don't know how
So I speed up and go without
And time runs out, as does the fuel
There's always one more job to do

Starting Over

From day one, you've been around
To scrape the pieces from the ground
Whenever I fell, and fall I did
But I'm no longer that same kid
I've grown a lot, and so have you
I've made mistakes, you've made some too
You tried so hard to make it work
Then grew apart and found new circles
Since you set each other free
A weight has been lifted from me
We all fail, and we all fall
But you have been you through it all

Checklist life

Get a job
Buy a home
Find a lover
Not alone
Check the boxes
Do the work
Find a new job
Ditch the jerk
Settle down, now
Don't forget
Your time is short
Unlike your debt
So have a child
It's the right way
Then have another
Start today!
Change your life
Then change it back
Quit your job
Get the sack
Lose your mind
Find your soul
That's what happens
As you grow

Mortal

One day I'll be something
I'll be someone, I'll be better

The next day, I'll be nothing
I'm just hoping they remember

One day, I won't worry
About all the days ahead

But until then, I'll be driven
By the timeline in my head

An Open Letter to Depression

You used to hold me down for hours
The weight of you would leave me powerless
Sometimes I wouldn't move for days
Drowning in a world of grey

I clawed my way out of your grasp
And wondered how long it would last
It's been years now, but I still relapse
A high like this always comes before a crash

One day I'll see you again
I hope I'm doing better then
So I'll remember what you did
And never fall back into your grip

Fortune Teller

Fortune teller
19 years old
Is this what you want forever?
Is there anyway to know?

Don't know where I'll be tomorrow
But I know I'll be with you
Can you really, truly promise?
I can do my best to be true

Simple Pleasures

When the grass is green and the sky is blue
Don't wait for red flags to come for you

When you've done the work and paid your dues
Don't be surprised when the wish comes true

When you see the way he's looking at you
Don't wonder if he's wanting somebody new

When there's money to make and work to do
Don't forget that time is more precious - it's true

Plastic

Your life looks so good online
Covered in makeup, guzzling wine
Keeping up with all the trends
Never letting the bar bend

Deep down, I want you have
All the glitz and all the glam
But it's not worth all the time
Makeup is a modern scam